FO

||||| ||| || |||| | ||||||| ||||||||||
W9-CGO-331

J
551.7   FO   R-3
M45   4.16

Maynard

The great ice age

DATE DUE			
DE 31 82			
AG 30 '83			
SE 17 '83			
JY 17 '84			
JY 30 '85			
AG 14 '85			
SE 4 '85			
AP 6 '88			
AG 23 '88			

GREAT RIVER REGIONAL LIBRARY
St. Cloud, Minnesota   56301

CONTENTS

THE GREAT ICE AGE

Christopher Maynard

Published 1979 by Warwick Press, 730 Fifth Avenue,
New York 10019
First published in Great Britain by Ward Lock in 1978
Copyright © 1978 by Grisewood & Dempsey Ltd
Printed in Italy by New Interlitho, Milan
6 5 4 3 2 1 All rights reserved

WARWICK PRESS · NEW YORK

Library of Congress Catalog Card No. 78–67833
ISBN 0–531–09128–7
ISBN 0–531–09113–9 lib. bdg.

Onslaught of the Cold

About two million years ago the climates of the world slowly began to change. Over the centuries, winters grew steadily colder and wetter, summers cooler and shorter. The world was entering the Great Ice Age.

As the temperature fell, the rolling northern grasslands gradually changed into pine forests. And as the grasslands disappeared, so did the animals that roamed them. Elephants, hyenas, cheetahs and jackals moved south to warmer lands. Their place was taken by woodland animals. In the new forests lived the Gallic moose and the bush-antlered deer. Here, too, roamed the fierce scimitar cat.

High on the upper slopes of mountain ranges, the snow and ice built up and formed the first glaciers. Throughout the long winters, blankets of fresh snow fell so thickly in the highlands that they no longer melted away in summer.

As time went on, more snow fell and the ice grew even thicker. Freezing winters were followed by cool summers when there was not enough warmth to melt the growing masses of ice.

In the lowlands, many trees and plants perished. Huge forests shrank into tiny clusters of hardy pines. And the creatures of the forest suffered. The biting cold and cruel blizzards drove them to find food and shelter wherever they could. Some crowded in caves. Others found refuge in sheltered valleys. And many of them died.

bush-antlered
deer

scimitar cat

5

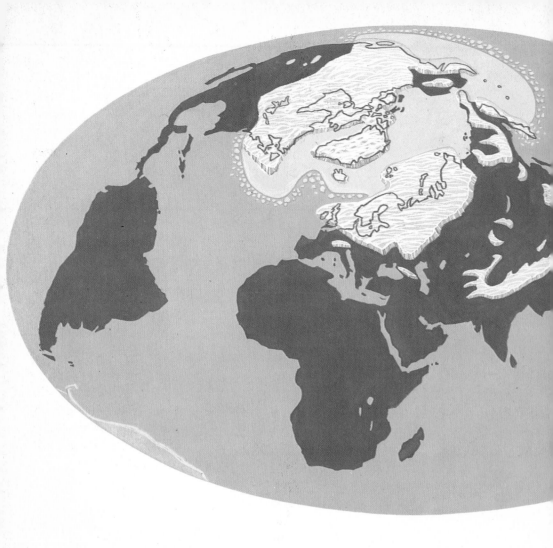

Ice on the March

Ice Age glaciers once covered nearly a third of the land surface of the Earth—an enormous area of over 17 million square miles. There were three great ice sheets: the Laurentian in America, the Scandinavian in Europe, and the Siberian in northeast Asia. The Laurentian was by far the largest. At its center over Hudson Bay it formed a high plateau over 3000 yards thick. From there it spread south more than 1500 miles to the present-day state of Missouri. In places the Laurentain glacier was so thick that even the tallest New York skyscrapers would have been buried deep beneath it.

Throughout the rest of the world, most high mountain ranges were capped by snowfields from which

Map showing the extent of the great ice sheets

Map showing the extent of the great ice sheets

glaciers spread out into the surrounding foothills and plains.

Ice Age glaciers changed the face of the land. Armed with rocks firmly embedded in the ice, the glaciers acted like gigantic files. They scraped out valleys thousands of miles long and ground down the tops of craggy mountains until they were smooth. Like great bulldozers, the moving glaciers picked up boulders the size of large houses and carried them along like pebbles. As the glaciers advanced, many millions of tons of rock and soil were shifted from one place to another. The present-day lowlands of Europe and North America are plastered with soil scraped from lands farther north during the Great Ice Age.

The picture below shows some of the scenery created by moving ice. A glacier has squeezed through a mountain valley, carving out steep sides and a flat floor. In the distance is a ridge of rock and soil dumped by the melting ice. Today a lake is trapped behind it. All that remains of the glacier is a small river winding along the floor of the valley.

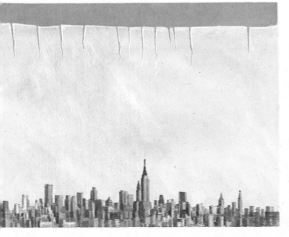

The Great Ice Age glaciers would have dwarfed the skyscrapers of New York.

The Glacier's Edge

As the great glaciers advanced across Europe and North America the pine forests disappeared in their path. They were replaced by vast treeless plains called tundras. Hardy creatures roamed these frozen wastes near the ice fronts, feeding on shrubs, mosses and lichens.

In America, bison and musk-oxen, mammoths and mastodons roamed ahead of the great ice sheets. They moved to regions that were once the home of saber-toothed cats and giant ground sloths—warmth-loving creatures that had moved even further south.

In Europe, the two-horned woolly rhino with its thick hairy coat lumbered over the barren tundra beside the giant woolly mammoth. And the giant deer with its huge shovel-like antlers searched the freezing land for grasses and shrubs.

From their bones, we know of other creatures that lived at the edge of the spreading glaciers—forest hogs, small shaggy horses, wolves, foxes and huge cave bears. All of these survived in the bitter cold of the Great Ice Age.

macaque

The Glaciers Retreat

The glaciers advanced four time
across North America and Europ
during the Great Ice Age. In betweer
there were warm spells, known a
interglacials, when the ice melted back

As the glaciers retreated, plantli
began to return to the land. First cam
the hardy shrubs and birches. Then, a
the climate warmed, they were fo
lowed by conifers and finally by fores
of oak and elm.

On two occasions, the climate be
came so warm that trees and shrub
even flourished in Spitzbergen. Th
island is far to the north of the Arcti
Circle. Today, it is permanently snow
covered.

hyena

In Europe, the climate was warmer
t times during the interglacials than
is today. It was warm enough for
ubtropical animals such as macaques
nd hippos to spread north of the Alps.
hey made their way into Germany,
nd even into the lowlands of southern
ingland, where hippos wallowed in
ne River Thames.

In the open woodlands that covered
much of the continent, wildlife teemed.
here was the fallow deer with its
cupped" antlers that were far bigger
han those of the modern deer. The
traight-tusked elephant, one of the
argest elephants ever, also made its
tome in northern Europe during the
nterglacials. Some of the other crea-
ures which thrived at this time in-
cluded bears, hyenas, lions, leopards
nd rhinoceroses.

elephant

fallow deer

The Deep Freeze

As the climate cooled at the close of each interglacial, the ice once again crept south. Most of the warmth-loving creatures were either driven to warmer lands or wiped out. Only the hardiest animals were able to survive the bitter cold that gripped America, Asia and Europe.

Nothing could live on the ice-cap itself. But many animals thrived in the great belt of tundra and forest to the south of the ice. Wherever river valleys gave some protection, cave lions and cave bears, wolves, reindeer, woolly rhinos and mammoths, bison and deer made their home. Here too lived Neanderthal Man.

Neanderthalers were short, less than four and a half feet tall on average. But they were very powerfully built. They clothed themselves in simple animal skins and used tools of bone and flint. When they went hunting, they carried knives, spears and stone axes. They lived by trailing after migrating reindeer herds. Or they stalked the woods in search of deer and wild cattle.

Neanderthalers often sheltered in caves and this is where most of their remains have been found. These show that the Neanderthalers were quite advanced people and not the simple man-apes they were once thought to be.

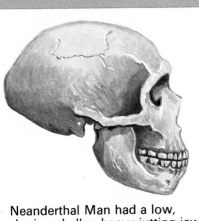

Neanderthal Man had a low, sloping skull, a heavy jutting jaw and a thick brow ridge. But his brain was larger than that of modern man.

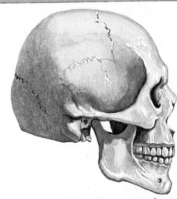

The skull of modern man has a high forehead, a rounded dome and a well-formed chin. This skull shape first appeared about 40,000 years ago.

If all the glaciers on Earth were to melt, the seas would rise by over 200 feet and flood the land. Europe would appear as it is shown on this map.

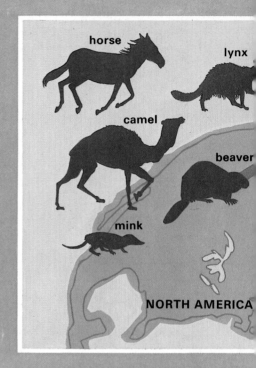

NORTH AMERICA

Land Bridges

As the glaciers advanced, billions of tons of water were frozen in ice-caps. The level of the oceans fell and great stretches of the sea-bed became dry land. Islands and continents that had been separated by water for millions of years now became linked by land bridges.

The most famous land bridge of all stretched from Asia to America. It crossed the area now known as the Bering Straits. When the land emerged from the sea here, it became a great highway for migrating wildlife. From Asia came shaggy musk-oxen, saber-toothed tigers, bison, bears, woolly mammoths and Man. From America, horses, camels, lynxes and mink moved into Asia.

During the warmest part of the Great Ice Age, forests grew on the Bering land bridge and woodland creatures like raccoons and beaver could make the crossing. At other times the land bridge was a bleak windswept tundra. Then, only the

bison

woolly
mammoth

Bering land
bridge

bear

musk ox

man

ASIA

hardiest grazing animals were able
to venture across.

This was the scene when the first
human beings from Asia crossed
into America some 25,000 to 40,000
years ago. They came in small hunting bands trailing behind wandering
herds.

15

Irish elk

mammoth

cave bear

woolly rhino

scimitar cat

The Doomed

Animals that could not stand the cold vanished very early during the Great Ice Age. But, mysteriously, many of the creatures which survived the worst cold suddenly died out just as the Ice Age ended.

The giant mammals were the hardest hit. About 30,000 years ago, many creatures such as the giant cave bears, scimitar cats, woolly rhinos, Irish elks and steppe mammoths became extinct. The reason for their strange disappearance may have been the rise of another animal. Towards the end of the Great Ice Age, Man became a skilled hunter.

In America, many kinds of animals vanished so quickly that it was as if a single great catastrophe had hit them. As recently as 11,000 years ago, most of the great beasts that had survived the cold still roamed the land.

The first creatures to disappear in North America were the great Shasta sloths, giant beavers and four-horned antelopes. Later, horses and camels died out, as did the mammoths. In South America, horses survived for a little longer. But by 8000 years ago, they too had vanished.

All over the world, the same thing was happening. Well-armed human hunters were slaughtering great numbers of animals. By the end of the Ice Age many creatures had completely disappeared.

camel

zebrine horse

Modern Man

During the last advance of the glaciers, Cro-Magnon man appeared. Cro-Magnons migrated into Europe from southwestern Asia around 35,000 years ago and began taking the place of the Neanderthalers who had been living there. Within 5000 years, Cro-Magnons were the only form of human being in the world. We are their direct descendants.

Cro-Magnons were very much at home along the fringes of the glaciers. They were very skilled tool-makers. They worked flints into superb knife blades, spearheads and arrowheads using wooden and bone hammers. From antlers and animal bones they carved spearheads, fish-hooks and spearthrowers.

To protect themselves from the bitter cold, they made warm animal-skin clothes using bone needles threaded with sinew. They often made their homes in caves. But when on the move after game, they lived in tents made of skins.

Cro-Magnon man was a skilled artist. Some of the fine drawings and paintings that he made can still be seen in caves all around Europe. Nearly all Cro-Magnon cave paintings are of animals and hunters.

Cro-Magnons also carved and decorated pieces of bone and antler. They loved to adorn themselves with bracelets and necklaces made from ivory, shells and teeth. Their clothes were also decorated with jewelry and ornaments.

Evidence of the Past

Fossils are remains of ancient animals. They are some of the best clues we have to what life was like in the past.

Some of the best Ice Age fossils have come from tar pits. These are formed when oil from within the Earth seeps to the surface. The oil collects in pools where it slowly turns into thick, sticky tar. When rain covers a tar pit with a thin layer of water, it becomes a deadly trap. Animals that come to drink become bogged down. The more they struggle, the worse they are trapped. Finally, they sink to their deaths. When the tar hardens, their bones are preserved as fossils.

The most famous tar pits of all are at Rancho La Brea in the middle of the city of Los Angeles in California. Thousands of creatures met their deaths here. Mastodons, bison, ground sloths, camels and horses all made their way to La Brea to drink. Once trapped in the tar, they became an easy meal for hunting and scavenging animals such as the dire wolf, the saber-tooth tiger, and the giant vulture. These animals in turn were lured into the sticky pools and sucked under.

wild horses

mastodon

The biggest member of the elephant family in North America was the emperor mammoth. It had long legs, a short body, huge curved tusks and large jaws. It stood over thirteen feet high at the shoulder.

vulture

golden eagle

dire wolves

saber-tooth tiger

21

Many animals became so used to the Ice Age cold that they retreated north with the ice as the weather became warmer. Today they live in parts of the world that most animals would find much too cold. Most of them are protected by thick fur or feathers. Some are also camouflaged white so that they seem to vanish against a snowy background.

The arctic hare, snowy owl, musk ox, reindeer and arctic fox are some of the animals that make their homes on the frozen treeless tundra. Other animals can live on the ice itself. Polar bears, seals and walruses all live on ice-floes. Nearly all their food comes from the sea since plants cannot grow on ice.

Last of all, there are groups of human beings who have learned how to live in the frozen north. The Lapps and the Eskimos both survive in the icy lands of the Arctic.